A Sister
Always...
A Friend Forever

That's my sister!
Love you Lynne!
Happy Birthday!

Love,
Kathy

1-11-08

Other Titles by Marci
Published by

Blue Mountain Arts®

Friends Forever
A Celebration of Friendship and Everything Friends Share
Through the Years

A Grateful Path
Inspirational Thoughts on Unconditional Love,
Acceptance, and Positive Living

To My Mother
Your Love Is a Lasting Treasure

Library of Congress Control Number: 2007902120
ISBN: 978-1-59842-250-4

Children of the Inner Light is a registered trademark. Used under license.

▐ and Blue Mountain Press are registered in U.S. Patent and Trademark Office.
Certain trademarks are used under license.

Printed in China.
First Printing: 2007

♻ This book is printed on recycled paper.

This book is printed on fine quality, laid embossed, 80 lb. paper. This paper has been specially produced to be acid free (neutral pH) and contains no groundwood or unbleached pulp. It conforms with all the requirements of the American National Standards Institute, Inc., so as to ensure that this book will last and be enjoyed by future generations.

Blue Mountain Arts, Inc.
P.O. Box 4549, Boulder, Colorado 80306

A Sister Always...
A Friend Forever

A Celebration of the Love,
Support, and Friendship
Sisters Share

Marci

Blue Mountain Press™
Boulder, Colorado

Introduction

Those of us who have sisters know that the sister relationship is one of the most special in our lives. In a sister, we are given the gift of someone who understands "who we are" and why. We are given the gift of a friend who loves us through the good times and bad and who sees the best in us even on the worst day.

Sisters have the unique opportunity to watch each other grow through a lifetime and to develop a deep connection based on family history, values, and common experiences. It is often only through time that sisters come to realize just how much they mean to each other. They come to understand that no other friend is quite like a sister, because she is the one who knows the path you've traveled and the dreams in your heart. She is there to answer your call for help... there to listen... and there in spirit even on the busiest day sending well wishes and hugs from her heart.

For all the special times you've shared with your sister... for all the precious, tiny moments locked in your heart... I hope these words give voice to your deepest feelings, enabling you to express the love and gratitude you feel for your sister. I hope, too, that you will give thanks for all the times you've had together — the triumphs and setbacks, the successes and losses, the good times and bad. Through this shared journey called sisterhood, you have experienced the greatest gift of all... love.

Marci

A Sister Always...
A Friend Forever

In childhood we did not understand the gift wrapped up in a greater plan. Time has taught us about the bond of love, and through that love we have chosen friendship. We have learned together, sharing the good times and the bad, and no matter what, there has always been love. You are my sister always, my friend forever.

The Bond
We Have Found
Is Everlasting

Our lives were brought together for a reason, and for that I am grateful. I have learned much from you, and you from me. We have loved and cried and found a bond that is everlasting. Thank you for your wisdom, strength, and hope and for always being there.

Not Everyone Is Lucky Enough to Have a Sister like You

We share a history that lets us understand each other. There is family that gives us a lasting connection of love, and there is a special closeness that has developed between us as we have shared life's journey. I am so thankful for you, my sister!

There's Something Extra Special About You

Some people have a way of brightening someone's day... and it's with the little things that mean so much. There is a phone call at just the right time, a hug when it is needed, or a comforting word of encouragement. That special person in my life is you!

You Always Know
Just What I Need

You've been a friend to me when I needed a friend... You've been a confidante when I needed to unburden my worries... You've been a mentor when I needed to be shown the way... You've been a bright light when I needed a brighter day. My life is so much better because of you and the memories that will live in my heart forever.

You Are Everything
I Could Ever Want
in a Sister and a Friend

When I want to talk... you listen. When I am down... you encourage me. When I am happy... you share my joy. When I am sad... your hug tells me that everything will be okay. You know my deepest hopes and share my greatest dreams.

I Know I Can Always
Count on You

Some days I just need a hand to hold… Some days I just need a hug… Some days I just need a word of encouragement… Some days I just need someone to be there for a laugh and a memory… On my "some days," there is you!

We Have Shared
So Much Through
the Years…

A sister shares life's journey with you, knowing where you come from as only a sister can... understanding what is in your heart as only a sister does... and loving you today and tomorrow as only a sister will.

♥

I Could Never Find
a Better Sister

If I searched the world, I could never find a better sister. You are a perfect example of sisterly love, care, compassion, and concern. Just talking to you can make me feel better. Your listening helps me sort out my thoughts, and hearing your perspective allows me to see things from a different point of view.

An Angel Must Have
Blessed My Life with You

Sometimes I wonder why I am so blessed to have a sister like you. You are always there... to help me fix the bad things, appreciate the little things, and remind me that the most important things in life are free. An angel must have blessed my life with you!

Only a Sister...

...remembers where you've been and shines a light of encouragement on the path before you.

...knows the love and happiness you share as family.

...is there with love, encouragement,
or a hug right when you most need it.

...can make a laugh so much better
and sorrow seem half as bad.

I'm So Glad
We Always
Have Each Other

Even though we are different in a lot of ways, we are alike in ways that are so important. Our values, our beliefs, and the things we hold dear — like family, love, and faith — create the ties that bind us. We can turn to each other in times of need... we support each other through life's challenges... and we share all the little blessings of life. I am so glad that we have each other.

If I Sometimes Forget to Say "Thanks" for All the Little Things You Do...

I want you to know that even when I do not say so, I am so thankful for your thoughtfulness, your caring, and your ability to give me hope in every situation. Your efforts never go unnoticed.

I Am So Grateful to
Have You
as My Sister

I want to be sure that you really know how much it means to me to have you as my sister. It's the simple things you do — that are so much a part of who you are — that mean so much... It's the way you walk beside me to share each day... the way you stand behind me when I question myself and walk in front of me when I've lost my way. You are such an important part of my life.

You Deserve the Best!

May all the good things you have brought to my life be returned to you.

May your guardian angel always watch over you and whisper life's secrets in your ear.

May your steps be guided through all of life's challenges and your heart remember its true calling.

May love warm your heart every day.

May your future be filled with love and acceptance.

Here's a
Hug

A sister's hug is worth
a thousand words.

Sister, I Am So Proud of You!

You have faced the challenges of life with courage, compassion, and conviction, and I am so proud of you. Thank you for sharing all that makes you special and everything you are with me.

You Have Taught Me
So Much

You have taught me that what
makes a "family" is not found in
a name; it is found in the heart.

You have taught me to face life
with courage and acceptance and
everything will work out as it should.

You have taught me that I can
believe in my dreams.

You have taught me that the things
that bring lasting happiness are faith,
hope, love, and the comfort of family
and friends.

You Are an Inspiration

Every day, you provide a
constant love that I depend on…
a quiet, steady, burning light that
inspires me to be my best.

Your Kind and Generous
Spirit Shines Brightly
in My Life

Some people change our lives without even realizing the impact they have made just by being themselves. Your special spirit has made such a difference in my life. I am grateful for the way you are always willing to share the precious gift of time... for always believing in the best in people... for always seeing the bright side of things... for the many kind words you have spoken... for the thoughtful things you have done... and for the way you are always there sharing the special person you are. The world needs more people like you!

There's One Thing That Will Never Change Between Us

I have watched you mature
and change through the years,
claiming "who you are" in your
search for the true meaning
of life. You should know that
through it all, the one thing that
has not changed, and never will,
is how much I care about you.

We Are Family

Time and the experiences of life have shown us a treasure that cannot be bought. We have a friendship built on the bonds of family... We know what is in each other's heart.

No Matter How Long
It Has Been Between Visits,
a Sister's Love Remains
Forever in Your Heart

Each time I see you, all time melts away. Precious moments come flooding back, and I am reminded of all the laughter and joy we have shared through the years. I am so appreciative of those times and of you.

A Sister's Love Blooms
Year After Year

Sister

A sister's love is a gift that you unwrap a little bit each year.

A sister is a mirror of things to come and a reflection of things gone by.

A sister shows you the road before you and knows the path you've taken.

A sister is the friend who has been there as long as your memories.

A sister is the one you call when you need to talk to someone who knows your heart.

A sister knows the things to say when life sends trials your way.

A sister knows how "you became you" because she was there!

A sister sees your beautiful spirit shining through on good days and bad.

A sister is a gift of friendship and family all wrapped up in love.

We Have the
Gift of
Each Other

We are fortunate to have someone who understands so much... who cares so much... who gives so much... who is so much fun to be with... who forgives mistakes... who is always willing to help... who is always there to listen... Thank you for the things that you give so freely and for being you!

We're Sisters!

When I think of you, I
think, "What could be better
than having someone to talk to
who already knows all about
me and loves me as I am?"

When I think of you, I think, "What could be more fun than sharing my joys with someone who is truly happy for me?"

When I think of you, I think, "What could be better than a friendship that has been a part of my life for as long as we've been sisters?"

When I think of you, I think, "We're sisters!" and I realize how lucky I am to share this wonderful gift with you.

These Are the Things
I Wish for You, Sister

I wish you a life filled with love… a true love to share your every dream… family love to warm your heart… and priceless love found in the gift of friendship.

I wish you peace... peace in knowing who you are... peace in knowing what you believe in... and peace in the understanding of what is important in life.

I wish you joy... joy as you awaken each day with gratitude in your heart for new beginnings... joy when you surrender to the beauty of a flower or a baby's smile... and joy, a hundred times returned, for each time you've brought happiness to another's heart.

You Are Always in My Heart

I wish life were not so busy... it is hard to believe how the days pass by with so much to do! Always remember how much you mean to me and that each and every day, no matter how busy I am or what is happening, you always have a place in my heart.

Sister,
I Love You

I am so happy that we have remained close through the years. Your love and support are gifts in my life, and your friendship is something I can count on. You are my sister always and my friend forever.

About Marci

Marci began her career by hand-painting floral designs on clothing. No one was more surprised than she was when one day, in a single burst of inspiration and a completely new and different art style, her delightful characters sprang from her pen! "Their wild and crazy hair is a sign of strength," she thought, "and their crooked little smiles are endearing." She quickly identified the charming characters as Mother, Daughter, Sister, Father, Son, Friend, and so on, until all the people and places in life were filled. Then, with her own loved ones in mind, she wrote a true and special sentiment to each one. This would be the beginning of a wonderful success story, which today still finds Marci writing each and every one of her verses in this same personal way.

Marci is a self-taught artist who has always enjoyed writing and art. She grew up working in her family's small grocery and sub shop. It was there, as she watched her dad interact with customers, she learned that relationships in the workplace and community, as well as in the family, provide the greatest satisfaction and joy.

She went on to develop a business from her home, making home-baked breads, cakes, and pastries to be sold in her dad's store. Later, she started another small home-based business hand-painting clothing for women. At first, she didn't have any idea she could paint and was amazed at how many people loved her work! She was gratified that she could create "wearables" that brought so much joy to those who wore them.

Now as she looks back, Marci sees how all her interests were pieces of a puzzle that fit together and gave her the skills she needed for her work today as artist and author. She is thrilled to see how her delightful characters and universal message of love have touched the hearts and lives of people everywhere.